Jersey Lilies

Soldiers Without a Name

A trilogy of plays

by

Anne Le Marquand Hartigan

CHISWICK BOOKS

LONDON

www.chiswickbooks.com

First published in 2016 by Chiswick Books
2 Prebend Gardens, Chiswick, London W4 1TW
email: info@chiswickbooks.com
website: www.chiswickbooks.com

Jersey Lilies copyright © Anne Le Marquand Hartigan 1996.

Anne Le Marquand Hartigan is hereby identified as author of this play in accordance with section 77 of the Copyright, Designs and Patents Act 1988. The author has asserted her moral rights.

All rights whatsoever in this play are strictly reserved and application for performance etc. should be made before commencement of rehearsal to email: rights@annehartigan.com. No performance may be given unless a licence has been obtained, and no alterations may be made in the title or the text of the play without the author's prior written consent.

This book is sold subject to the condition that it shall not by way of trade or otherwise be circulated without the publisher's consent in any form of binding or cover or circulated electronically other than that in which it is published and without a similar condition including this condition being imposed on any subsequent purchaser.

British Library Cataloguing in Publication Data. A catalogue record for this book is available from the British Library.

ISBN: 978-1-910721-02-5

Cover image from a painting by Anne Le Marquand Hartigan.

'Hey, Little Hen' Music and Words by Noel Gay and Ralph Butler
© Copyright 1941 Chester Music Limited trading as Noel Gay Music Company, worldwide rights except the United Kingdom, Ireland, Australia, Canada, South Africa and all so-called

reversionary rights territories where the copyright © 1994 is held jointly by Chester Music Limited trading as Noel Gay Music Company and Chest Music Limited trading as Campbell Connelly & Co. Limited. All Rights Reserved. International Copyright Secured. Used by permission of Chester Music Limited trading as Noel Gay Company and Chester Music Limited trading as Campbell Connelly & Co. Limited.

'Run, Rabbit, Run' Music by Noel Gay, Words by Noel Gay & Ralph Butler © Copyright 1939 Chester Music Limited trading as Noel Gay Music Company, worldwide rights except the United Kingdom, Ireland, Australia, Canada, South Africa and all so-called reversionary rights territories where the copyright © 1994 is held jointly by Chester Music Limited trading as Noel Gay Music Company and Chester Music Limited trading as Campbell Connelly & Co. All Rights Reserved. International Copyright Secured. Used by permission of Chester Music Limited trading as Noel Gay Company and Chester Music Limited trading as Campbell Connelly & Co. Limited.

'It's a Hap Hap Happy Day-Cues' Words and Music by Sammy Timberg and Winston Sharples © 1941, Reproduced by permission of Sony/ATV Harmony, London W1F 9LD.

'Teddy Bears Picnic' Words and Music by Jimmy Kennedy and John W Bratton © 1907, Reproduced by permission of B Feldman & Co Ltd/ M Witmark & Sons/ EMI Music Publishing Ltd, London W1F 9LD.

Also by the author

Plays

Beds, *Chiswick Books, 2016*
I Do Like To Be Beside The Seaside, *Chiswick Books, 2016*
La Corbière, *Chiswick Books, 2016*
Three Short Plays, *Chiswick Books, 2016*
The Secret Game, *Chiswick Books, 2014*

Poetry

Unsweet Dreams, *Salmon Poetry, 2011*
To Keep The Light Burning, *Salmon Poetry, 2008*
Nourishment, *Salmon Poetry, 2005*
Immortal Sins, *Salmon Poetry, 1993*
Now is a Moveable Feast, *Salmon Poetry, 1991*
Return Single, *Beaver Row Press, 1986*
Long Tongue, *Beaver Row Press, 1982*

Prose

Clearing the Space, *Salmon Poetry, 1996*

For Robert Gordon for his work with me on the production, and for all my Jersey relations, especially those who suffered the German occupation.

First performed by Moveable Feast Theatre Company at the
Samuel Beckett Theatre, Dublin, 1996 with the following cast:

La Corbière

All parts played by Anne Le Marquand Hartigan

WOMAN

WHORE

Le Crapaud

All parts played by Robert Gordon

VOICE

THE NICE WOMAN

THE NAZI OFFICER

THE SLAVE

WOMAN

Les Yeux

All parts played by Anne Le Marquand Hartigan and
Robert Gordon

SUZANNE

LUCY

THE EYE

NAZI ONE

NAZI TWO

THE ABORTION

THE BIG BAD WOLF

BETRAYER ONE

BETRAYER TWO

KURT

NAZI UNIFORM

NURSE

Directors	Robert Gordon and Anne Le Marquand Hartigan
Production Manager	Dominic Hartigan
Production Consultant	Cathy Leeney
Costumes	Mary Donnelly
Lighting	Hugh Hartigan
Lighting Operator	Dave Marsh
Audio Production	Marion McEvoy
Photography	Hugo Glendinning

Notes on the plays

It's quite possible to produce parts two and three as a two-act play. When Robert Gordon and I did the production in Dublin, I had the desire to bring La Corbière back to the original poem itself, and did this by acting it as a one-woman piece. The other two short plays are both based on incidents that happened on the island of Jersey during the Nazi occupation. I felt it was important that they should be recorded and chose the surrealist style as it was the way the artist, Claude Cahun, constructed her photographs and other works. Cahun and Suzanne Malherbe were brave and remarkable women and their opposition to the oppression and cruelty of the Nazis was important. They deserve recognition. Hopefully these plays, based on their work and letters, will help raise awareness of their role.

One

La Corbière

There is an account of the arrival and departure of a boatload of French women, prostitutes, shipped to the island of Jersey in the Channel Islands during World War

II by the German Army for their soldiers' entertainment. None of these women was young. They remained on the island for a year or maybe two. They were not used. Then they were herded into coasters to be shipped back to Normandy. The ships were wrecked off La Corbière lighthouse on the very rocky coastline. Nearly all the women were drowned. Their bodies were left in the sea and were seen for days, sometimes alone, sometimes in clusters, their peroxide hair floating out on the waves.

Two

Le Crapaud

At the same time as the La Corbière incident in the early 1940s, there were people on the island of Jersey and the other islands who were working for the Nazis and treated as slaves. These men were controlled by the Organisation Todt, or OTs, as they were called. The slaves came from all over Europe and were kept without proper rations and slowly starved. They were treated brutally by the OTs. Many died. The slaves built defences and the underground hospital at St Laurence in Jersey where this play is set. Nowadays, this hospital is a tourist attraction, and it is no longer noted in the brochure that inside the walls of the hospital there are the remains of slaves who died working there, whose bodies were incorporated into the walls of the hospital as it was built. This part of the Jersey Lilies trilogy starts with a woman in contemporary time in the underground hospital, then moves back in time to 1941-42 to a German officer in the same location, then to a Russian.

N.B. The people of Guernsey nickname the Jersey people 'les crapauds' or 'toads.'

Three

Les Yeux - The Eyes

The final play in the trilogy is based on the lives and writing of two extraordinary women, Claude Cahun (Lucy) the French surrealist photographer/artist/writer and her step-sister, Suzanne Malherbe, who carried out their own unique, brave and humorous form of resistance to the Nazi occupation.

Extracts from the letters of Claude Cahun are included with grateful thanks to Basil Bigg. All reasonable attempts have been made to contact the copyright holders of Claude Cahun's letters in order to seek permission to publish extracts. You are invited to contact info@chiswickbooks. com if you are the copyright holder.

Background notes

In the Dublin performance, only two actors were used for all three plays: a one-woman play; a one-man play; and a two hander. This happened through the development of the play itself. To start out, I wished to return to the original poem, La Corbière, and act it as a one-woman piece. Robert Gordon directed me in this 'new' La Corbière and this led me to write a one-man play for him, Le Crapaud, to go with La Corbière. In Le Crapaud, Gordon played a female as well as male characters. This, in turn, led me to write the final play, Les Yeux. Keeping the unity of the form of development of the first two plays, I continued with two actors who play all parts, which, in turn, brought about innovative and adventurous structures. I wanted a surreal and humorous quality to Les Yeux because this reflects the art of Cahun (Lucy) which is full of powerful imagery and humour. A woman taking on the Nazi uniform highlights, but at the same time, removes us from the cliché of Nazism. It raises and examines the idea and nature of all kinds of uniform, army, Nazi, prostitute...

This play can be performed with more actors, making gender swapping unnecessary, although I think the first two plays should stay as solo performances. It might be interesting to cast Les Yeux with two women actors.

The story behind the title, Jersey Lilies, is that the Germans brought Hitler Youth to the island for propaganda purposes. The girls went around in white dresses and were called Jersey Lilies by the local population as a form of derision. There is a flower, unique to Jersey, called the Jersey Lily. There was also the famous actress and beauty, and Jersey native, Lillie Langtry. Lilies are also associated with the dead.

Anne Le Marquand Hartigan

One

La Corbière

Characters

All parts played by one woman

WOMAN

WHORE

Scene One

The play begins in darkness. Sound of crashing waves. There is a rock centre stage with a coat draped over it and a swathe of white silk which spreads from the rock, widening to downstage. A pair of high heeled shoes lie downstage.

There is a rough wooden cross upstage left as on slaves' and prisoners' graves. WOMAN sits on a rock with her back to the audience.

WOMAN speaks in darkness, light slowly rising during her first speech. Light from La Corbière Lighthouse pans around and flashes into the eyes of the audience.

WOMAN

    Corbière   Corbière   Corbière

       Hair air   Hair air   air air air

    Corbière bier   Corbière bier   Corbière bier

    Requiem aeternam dona eis domine

    Corpus   Christi   Corpus   Christi

Lights up.

WOMAN half-turns.

    Lot   their lot   got their lot   Deserved

Their lot   harlot harlot   harlot harlot

WOMAN swings around suddenly.

WHORE

Rise up ye strong whores.   RISE.

WHORE WHORE WHORE

    WHORE WHORE WHORE

        WHORE WHORE WHORE.

Har lot Har lot Har lot   Har lot Har lot Har lot

Rise up ye strong whores.

Sisters rise up   Strong.

Strong Sisters

Wronged Sisters.

I will weep for thee

mourn for thee

cry for thee

in the strong salt sea will long for thee

sing for thee   sea sister   water sister

we will howl for thee

banshee for thee

weep for thee   as the salt sea seep for thee

Sinks down and lies over rock, as if drifting, floating in the sea, rocking with the words on voice-over.

slop   clop   clop   flop   smack   lack   back

the rock teeth   the rock teeth   the teeth

the grate grind grit growl   the suck back

shoal grawl   hiss hawl   hiss hawl   hiss hawl

gravel drawl   drawldown   suckback   back

WHOOOORRRE.

Blackout. End of voice-over.

WOMAN walks downstage right. Spotlight on WOMAN.

Nothing,

There is nothing.

Nothing but the sea.

Straight.   Flat.   Empty.   Iron.

Terrible as tin.

A lining fallen from the grey sky.

Nothing.

All barbarities buried.

The rock teeth and ripped flesh.

Turns back on audience.

Our tears are salt   and the sea,

the sea salt   and our tears

         weep

weeping the sea salt   and our tears

weeping the salt   from the sea

salt   salt   salt   Assault

*As if hit in the back on the word 'assault',
blackout and strobe light showing WOMAN
fighting and resisting attack in different poses,
ending on the rock, centre stage. Meanwhile the
following on voice-over:*

assault   rape   salt   rape   sea

seasalt   rapesalt

rapesalt   weep   asleep   dead

beat   beat   dead

beatdead   beatdead   beatdead

salt   salt   salt   salt   salt

Bereft   Bereft   Bereft

WOMAN mimes contentment playing with the white silk that lies over the rock.

Marriage   home   Mother   child

good   sweet   clean   bread   home

bed   sheetswhite   Mother

now   found   safe   clean

safe   bread   found   soft

warm mother   Baby pink   clean

sweet   home   soft   good   warm

when   now   safe   always   together

        Pure Good

warm bread   white now   food

warm cosy   Mother sister   child

gentle   good   Holy   now gentle

never soft   always good   always

always   all ways   all   ways

ways   ways   ways

With fear in her voice.

ways

    ways

End of voice-over.

Apart   Gap

Broken   open   now   alert

Not   alert   Not now   please

Stop.   No.   Not   That.

Here.   Don't.   Please   stop

Don't   NO   Not that

Mothersaid   pleasedon't

No not.   I don't

Is fighting off attacker, lying on the floor struggling.

Varies voice with each phrase, from deep to light to childlike to representing both the violater and the victim.

Like this   Like this

    Like this   Like this

Likethis   Likethis

    Like this   Not that

Like this   Notthat   Like this

Notthat   Like this   Notthat

Not that

Deep voice.

that   that   that   that   that

Light voice.

this   this   this   this   this

Deep voice.

that   that   that   that   that

Is thrown aside, face down.

WHORE

She recovers, heals.

Shore Whore Shore Whore Swell Shore

Whore drawl Sea Shore Whore child

Sand Sea Swell Sea Sea Sea Sea Stone Rock

Sea swellchild Swell with child Swell with sea

Swell with stone Swell with sea Swell with stone.

There is no answer but stone.

*Blackout. Voice-over. Alternating lights up and
blackout during the following 'sand' section.
Each time the lights go up, WOMAN is discovered
in a different position as if discarded and washed
up by the sea.*

sand   sand   sand   sand   sand   sand

sand   sand   sand   sand   sand
sand   sand   sand   sand   sand   sand
   sand   FOOT   sand   sand   sand
sand   sand   sand   LOVE   sand   sand
   sand   BREAST   sand   sand   sand   sand
sand   sand   sand   sand   BELLY   sand
   sand   sand   sand   sand   sand   sand
sand   CUNT   sand   sand   sand   sand
   sand   LOVE   sand   sand   sand   sand
sand   sand   sand   sand   sand   sand
   SHIT   sand   Rock   sand   Rock   sand
Rock   sand   slit   rock   crunch   sand
   rock   sand   sand   sand   sand   sand
sand   sand   sand   sand   rockabye   sand
sand   rock   sand   a-bye   sand   baby   sand
sand sand BREAST sand sand BABY sand
sand sand BREAST sand sand BABY sand
sand sand sand SLIT ROCK HAND BREAST

FOOT BELLY THIGH FLESH

SMELL ROT GUT ROT

sand   sand   sand   sand   sand   sand
   sand   sand   sand   sand   sand   sand

sand BONE sand sand FINGER sand MOUTH
sand sand sand LIPS sand SMELL sand
TASTE sand sand DRY sand sand sand
WIND sand sand COLD DRY COLD DRY
sand sand sand sand sand
COLD WET WILD COLD DRY BABY
BREAST FOOT MOUTH LIPS BREAST
BELLY CUNT LOVE CUNT BREAST
LIPS MOUTH COLD

DRY sand bone DEAD BREAST sand sand
BREAST ROT BLUE MOULD GUT ROT SAND
sand sand sand sand sand sand
sand sand sand sand sand sand
sand sand sand sand sand sand
sand sand sand sand sand sand
sand sand sand san san sa
sa sa sa s s s s s s s

End of voice-over. WOMAN lies off rock, head down.

GATHER KEEP STAY HOLD BELONG TRUST

Sits.

      trust   collect   hoard   hold   stay

Be   long   be   long   long   stay   keep

      trust be long   trust   Always

All   ways   Always   trust   keep

Holds her body possessively.

      touch be long mine   mine   mine

mine   mine   mine   mine   MINE

Blackout.

Light on WOMAN standing front right.

The sea lies flat as tin.

Flat as lies told down the black telephone receiver.

The sea lies flatter than the earth, its mouth tight shut on the night sky. The sky cannot penetrate and the clouds

Blot out the moon.

An ink stain on grey.   Nothing.   No where.

This is not.   Negative.   Finished.   Silence.

No gull cry.

No sea sound.

The iron lid is on.

The steel grey lid on the sea.

Bolted down with rust.

The sea is nailed to the shore   the moon at last is powerless.   Nailed down

it cannot scream or flap.

Every still wave and water-rivel

finished.

The last paper bag blown.

The last bottle sucks in its sides.

The last black salted shoe loses a sole.   Night Over.   Finished.   Taboo.   Taboo.   Taboo.

The sea is bolted down, racked, drawn tight in a rictus smile,

Under this grey teeth of waves   they are buried.

They are finished.

They are scrubbed out.

Turns to walk upstage and turns again, facing audience.

Not known at this address, this watery arbour, this stiff sea

Where the rocks' teeth lie, in unison, chorus, dateline.

Becomes WHORE. Sits on rock.

WHORE

>Ripped.　　Eaten.　　Digested.　　Afloat in
>a shark's belly.　　A lunch for lobsters.
>The eyeballs float apart.　　The peroxide
>hair slimed.　　Teeth and nose bridges litter
>the floorbed　　your seabed　　your last bed
>What the fuck?　　Who the fuck?　　We were
>fucking professionals of fuck　　fish fuck
>
>*Walks downstage, challenging, puts feet into high heeled shoes.*
>
>Your lovers.　　Your time-machines.
>Your nothings.　　Your holes.
>Your forgetting.　　　　Your guilt-holder.
>Your silences.　　Your dirt.　　Your rubbish.
>Your hate.　　Your violence.
>Your punchball.　　Your face, your Mother.
>Your enemy,　　your lies,　　your memory,
>Your toilet,　　your headache,　　your madness,
>Your money.　　YOURS.　　Your expense account.
>Your throw-away.　　Your useless.　　Your dustbin.
>Your disposable.　　Your waste.　　Possessed.

Owned for an hour.   Bought.   Sold.
Less than cattle.   Herded.
Walks upstage, back to audience, picks up the coat from the rock and swings it on.
Voice-over.
Rock and flow.

In clusters your bodies dance,
together you're flowers, yellow
hair spread on the sea's time.

Rock and flow.

For a time you rest on the skim
of the sea, balanced over
rock cavities.

No one is coming.
End of voice-over.
WOMAN moves swiftly and smoothly downstage to stage front.
No one is coming with arms to dip

No strong arms to dip down you out from

The sea's terror.   No one.

No white arms over the boat's side

To reach over the edge.

No one is searching.   No eyes

Eager as searchlights   as La Corbière light

Sweeps its inevitable arc over the storm.

WOMAN turns upstage, lights a candle and turns during the next three lines. Kneels as if at the head of one of the dead. Lights very low.

No one will lay you out in a quiet room.

No one will light a candle at your head and feet.

There will be no prayers.

No one will push their boat out to

Take your bodies back to earth.

You bob your last dance on the sea's foam,

Flotsam,   rock and flow,

Spread-eagled on the indifferent sea.

Stands.

No chrism to anoint your brow,

No incense around your coffin of wood,

No name in the newspaper,

No name.

Sorrow is a lost word.

There are no tears,

Can the salt sea weep?

Only a harsh gull's cry.

Silence. Blows out the candle. Blackout.

Two

Le Crapaud

Characters

All parts played by one man

VOICE

THE NICE WOMAN

THE NAZI OFFICER

THE SLAVE   civilian, possibly a Russian

WOMAN

Scene One

There is a rock, centre stage, with a coat draped over it and a swathe of white silk which spreads from the rock, widening to downstage - as for La Corbière. Downstage a bundle of rags, clothes, to give the feeling of, and to look like, a body with arm extended. A shovel. A telephone.

Lighting continuously changing throughout: torch-light/ black-out/match-strike/candle/black-out/flash of bright light/black-out. Lights from different directions, high up and at floor level, upstage and downstage, playing with space, creating underground, making other space than the voice, sometimes approaching and sometimes receding.

Semi-dark or light as from afar, as in the light at the end of a tunnel or light from under the cloth. VOICE might be heard from telephone picked up by THE NICE WOMAN, or an answer-phone, or voice-over.

VOICE

> *Recorded and played as voice-over. Actor stands in silence in blackout and flashes torch intermittently.*
>
> Stone
>
> > Axe

Deep breath.

        Stone

        Axe

Deep breath.

            Stone

Deep breath.

              Stone

              Axe

Deep breath.

                  Stone

Deep breath.

Breathing (deep breaths).

Pause.

Breathing (deep breaths).

Pause.

Spoken as if the voice were hacking at stone.

                  AXE

                  AXE

                  AXE

Pause.

Blackout.

    AXE

Breathing.

Torch flash.

Breathing.

AXE

Breathing.

AXE

Pause.

Breathing.

Pause. Sound of body falling.

Stone

The word 'Stone' to be drawn out to last up to 10 seconds.

Scene Two

THE NICE WOMAN, a tourist, is visiting the underground hospital with her family. Lights up on THE NICE WOMAN dressed in raincoat and scarf, seated back to audience.

THE NICE WOMAN
>Peculiar.
>
>That's what it is, Joe. Peculiar.

Pause.

I wish I hadn't eaten that ice. I do.

I wish I hadn't.

As if to a child.

Hold my hand Sylvia, there's a good girl. Mind your feet.

Pause.

Of course it wouldn't have been all clean like this, I suppose. Well, when it was built it was clean, because it was a hospital. Ugh. Down here in a tunnel. Not very nice really. Not nice. But clever, you have to give them that. Very clever. The Nazis.

Oh look. These models are really life-like. Look Sylvie, that's the surgeon, that's the nurse. They're doing an operation. No, love. To make him better, to make the soldier better. They are helping him to get better. No they're not puppets, they are models, made of wax I expect or plastic, plastic it would be, wouldn't it Joe?

Pause.

That's a nasty story, Joe. I don't really care for that. A bit creepy. It looks so ordinary now. Yes

Sylvia, you're right, a bit like the underground at home.

Pause.

They went down there to be safe from the Huns.

Pause.

The Germans were Huns. The Nazis.

Pause.

They dropped bombs.

Pause.

On us. In London and other places.

Pause.

Well, because we were at war.

Pause.

We were fighting the Huns.

Pause.

Nazis.

Pause.

Germans. And they were fighting us.

Pause.

They started it.

Pause.

Oh, yes, we dropped back on them.

Pause.

They built this to be safe from…

Pause.

Yes. Well…

Pause.

Yes, that's a Nazi doctor mending a Hun's leg.

Pause.

To make him better, darling.

Pause.

To drop more bombs?

Pause.

Well…

Pause. She laughs.

Yes. No. Well. Oh.

Changes the subject.

Let's see what's in here, shall we…?

I'd rather you shut up, Joe. I don't want to know about that. It's not nice to think of that at all. Bodies shovelled in behind these walls.

Pause.

That can't be true.

Creepy.

Pause.

Shut up, Joe. It's not nice to know about things like that. The Jersey people were very brave. Makes it seem a little better.

Pause.

I've had enough of this. My stomach is just not right since that ice. Sort of heavy.

Pause.

Let's go up. I've had enough. We can come back another day to see the rest. I know it cost three fifty each, Joe, but, well, you can't tell how you're going to feel until you try something.

Pause.

VOICE

    Whispering.

    Breath   Stone

THE NICE WOMAN

    How they've done it

VOICE

    Breath   Stone

THE NICE WOMAN

    True to life

VOICE

    Stone   Breath

THE NICE WOMAN

    Clever

    Voice-over sound of long slow breath.

    A nice cup of tea, that's the thing to make me better.

    Freeze.

    THE NICE WOMAN now removes her coat and scarf to become THE NAZI OFFICER during the construction of the underground hospital. The end of Scene Two moves into Scene Three seamlessly.

Scene Three

Lights low.

THE NAZI OFFICER

    Swings around and walks downstage.

    Organisation is the need of daily life.

    Pause.

Order is the mark of civilized people.

We know the value of true discipline.

Human civilisation is based on the concept of discipline. It is the foundation of our humanity. With it we bring order to nature.

Order is the mark of humanity. We are human and civilised.

The clean sweep of order is our style.

Order once established means harmony. Peace.

Pause.

The realisation of these simple facts would save so much trouble.

These are soft islands.

Dots in the sea.

Pebbles merely

thrown overboard,

flipped in by some casual god

skimming stones across time.

Pause.

The centre is rock.

Resistant. Tough. Resistant to seas, to

axe, to blast, to drill.

Resistant.

We worm in.

Out.

Over there. Across over there. Out of here. Here is nothing.

This puny island.

Insignificant. Petty.

Pause.

Those islands out there wait for us.

Pause.

To look.

Look, there. The swallows. The house martins. They cluster on the roofs, stringing the wires, ordering the young ones. Giving directions.

Pause.

They can go. Ready. Steady.

Claps hands.

Go, go, go.

Marches up and down. Speaks as if emphasising control and dominance of the Nazis.

Correct. Right. Orderly. Discipline.

Power. Order. Control. Order. Rules. Correct.

Boot. Power. Power. Boot. Obey. Command.
Obey. Command. Obey. Power. Power. Power.
Boot.

Boot. Boot. Boot. Boot. Boot.

Silence.

Sings to the tune of Run Rabbit Run.

> Run rabbit, run rabbit, run, run, run.
>
> Don't let the farmer have his fun, fun, fun.
>
> He'll get by without his rabbit pie.
>
> So run rabbit, run rabbit, run, run, run.

Silly English song.

Sees the body.

I don't, in any way, go along with this sort of thing.

This is just not the way to run things along correct lines.

To be totally honest. To be totally frank, I'm sorry. I have to say, that if I had my way, this is not the way I would do things. I, of course, have no say in the matter, being a junior officer I accept.

But things like this mean something is out of order.

Sometimes, it seems that the system gets out of control.

Discipline. Order. Right.

Simple words, simple concepts. Necessary. Important.

Civilised. It angers me this sort of thing. Not necessary.

Pokes the body with his foot.

It pains me to see this stupidity. This waste.

Moves down to kneel beside body.

Tender   flesh   feather   bone

Temple   blue   skin   wrinkle   tender

Light   air   left   gone   socket   slight

Fragile frail tissue warm cold nothing. Thing

Stands up, moves away.

Only a thing.

With amusement.

The OT bashed his brains out with a spade,
they chucked his body in the cavity in the wall.
Stone. Dig him in, they laughed. Stone. Say your
prayers. Stone. R.I.P. Stone. R.I.P. R.I.P. Stone.
Cover him up. Stone. Keep him warm. Stone, he's
still warm, almost, stone.

Goes right and takes out notepad and ticks off list as he reads.

Marine M3.1 bayonet and scabbard

Pray for us

M98 Mauser rifle 7.0 with bayonets and scabbards

Pray for us

M98 Mauser 70s

Pray for us

Schmeisser MP40, 9mm, machine pistols

Pray for us

Pouches for 7.0 ammunition

Pray for us

BRNO light machine guns

Pray for us

7.9 Rifle ammunition

Pray for us.

Turns page.

Motor cycle goggles

Have mercy on us

Iron Cross, 2nd class, with swords

Have mercy on us

M42 gas masks

Have mercy on us

Armour piercing shells

Have mercy on us

20mm anti-aircraft shells

Have mercy on us

20mm anti-aircraft armour piercing shells

Grant us peace

Turns page.

Nazi armbands

Pray for us

Luger PO8, 9mm, automatic pistols

Pray for us

Walter P38, 9mm, automatic pistols

Pray for us

Etienne revolvers, 9mm,

Pray for us

Browning pistols, 9mm,

Pray for us

Mauser pistols, 6.350

Pray for us

Air force dress daggers and scabbards pray for us

> Pistols, holsters
>
> Forgive us our sins
>
> Dress bayonet and toggles
>
> Grant us eternal rest
>
> May perpetual light
>
> Shine upon us.
>
> Amen.

Puts away notebook. Goes to camp stool and removes uniform while singing.

> Run rabbit, run rabbit, run, run, run.
>
> Here comes the farmer with his gun, gun, gun
>
> Bang, bang, bang, goes the farmer's gun,
>
> So run rabbit, run rabbit, run, run, run.

THE NAZI OFFICER removes his boots and coat and he becomes THE SLAVE. He is in a truck on a train travelling somewhere across Europe. Light drops to blackout, then comes up brutally, white spot on THE SLAVE's face. THE SLAVE sits facing audience where he sat as THE NICE WOMAN.

WOMAN in dress, as prostitute is half seen in profile stage right.

WOMAN

> *Sings the first three lines of 'White Cliffs of Dover.' Light fades. WOMAN exits.*

Scene Four

THE SLAVE working underground during the construction of the hospital. Harsh spotlight on THE SLAVE.

THE SLAVE

> So many of us. Crowded into trucks. Packed in. Stuffed in. Kept there for a month. Sitting in our shite. Where else.
>
> Shunted across Europe.
>
> *Pause.*
>
> Food? Oh, ha, ha. Black bread. Soup?
>
> Water.
>
> *Pause.*
>
> Some of us could not walk for weakness when we got to St Malo.
>
> *Stands and moves downstage.*
>
> Now, here I am, on this holiday island.

Pause.

Same clothes on me.

I am a shit bag.

Pause.

The food, worse.

Makes as if hewing rock.

Stone   stone   stone

Stone   stone   stone

Stone   stone   stone.

This is not a place.

Hews rock.

Stone   stone   stone.

This is not a place at all.

Hews rock.

Stone rock   stone rock   stone rock.

This is not a place I would come to.

Goes to his own tunnel space. Squats, rocks, thinks.

They buried me before I died.

Throws grain for imaginary chickens.

They have buried me before already.

Talks to the hens.

Butch butch butch butch.

Chuck chuck chuck chuck.

Pause.

Pride and joy.

The chickens were my mother's pride and joy.

Pause.

Sings.

> Hey little hen,
>
> When, when, when
>
> Will you lay me an egg
>
> For my tea?

Pause.

I was sent out to bring them in, the chickens.

How they'd scatter, all over the place,

high and low, scratchy, scratchy.

Sings.

> Get into your nest,
>
> Do your little best,
>
> Get it off your chest,
>
> I can do the rest.

Pause.

I keep on dying here.

Pause.

That is all I am good at.

That is all I am good for.

To the hens.

Chuck chuck.

I will become perfect.

Dead perfect.

A pearl of death.

As if mimicking Lord Haw Haw.

Germany calling.

As self.

Knit one,

slip one,

pearl two together.

As if mimicking Lord Haw Haw.

Germany calling.

As self.

Knit one,

slip one,

pearl two together.

As if mimicking Lord Haw Haw.

Germany calling.

As self.

Knit one,

slip one,

pearl two together.

I am stink

I am shell

A flapping rag

A smelling hole.

To the hens.

Brown eggs. White eggs.

Little black hen

Comb, blood red,

eggs white as snow.

Thinking of a girl.

Lips as red as blood.

Cheek as soft as an angel's wing.

Fade to whisper.

Sings softly.

> Sweetheart, sweetheart
>
> Will you love me ever?

Prays.

Hail Mary, full of grace, the Lord is with thee,

Blessed art thou amongst women

And blessed is the fruit of thy womb...

Knit one,

slip one,

pearl two together.

My mother.

Sings.

> Hail, Queen of Heaven,
>
> The Ocean's Star,
>
> Guide of the wanderer
>
> Here below,
>
> Thrown on life's surge,
>
> We claim thy care,
>
> Save us from peril
>
> And from woe.
>
> Virgin most pure,
>
> Star of the sea,
>
> Pray for the wanderer,
>
> Pray for me.

Stops singing.

I am piss

I am bone

Dung my flesh

A worm's home.

Silence.

In the beginning there was pong.

Shite. Am shite. Am stink. Urine. Turds.

I escaped from the camp. Hid down in the ditch,

crouched dead-down beside the hen-house.

The little chuckling hens, I could hear them.

They smelled me out.

They found me. Helped me. Hid me. Fed me.

Three eggs, bread, coffee,

three eggs, bread, coffee.

Water. I washed. Took my rags, burnt them.

My head was alive. Walking. Eaten with lice.

In the morning, the bed black with the creatures.

I minded the hens.

I had to move. Eyes everywhere.

Pause.

Every night a different pillow.

Move. Move.

So Jerry wouldn't twig.

Some got away with it.

Pause.

Back in the shite.

Sings the first three lines of 'White Cliffs of Dover.'

Even without eyes, the rocks have seen too much.

Silence.

On the rocks the limpets cling. For thousands of years the limpets have clung.

Pause.

All they achieve is survival.

Pause.

We tried to eat raw limpets.

Pause.

My poor comrades. Oh my poor comrades. The OTs for their fun, oh ha, their fun, they marched you off the end of the pier...

Pause.

because you ate raw limpets, just for their fun.

Pause.

Laughing. Silence.

We have no rocks to cling to.

Sings the first three lines of 'White Cliffs of Dover.'

Then as if beckoning hens.

Chuck chuck chuck chuck.

Butch butch butch butch.

Come here, come here, come here, pretty yellow feet.

I know you. You are hiding your eggs on me, away in the grass.

Pause.

Forgive me, little black hen, your one white egg.

Comes out of his tunnel and works with his axe or shovel.

Rock hard stone hard breath.

Rock hard stone hard breath.

Repeat the above lines as needed. Slave rests on shovel, or could continue shovelling in time with the rhyme, or a mixture of both.

A young lad let his pigeon off

Gave him to the air,

Message on his little leg,

All set fair.

Someone told the Jerries

Someone told the Hun.

Jerry was so very cross

He didn't think it fun.

So they shot him

Bang, bang, bang.

Just seventeen he was,

Who gives a hang?

Works.

Rock hard   stone hard   rock hard

Rock hard   stone hard   rock hard.

Food. Mad for it.

Food.

Grip gripe belly bowel

Shitters squitters shaking...

He walks as if queuing for food, carrying a bowl.

Stand in a queue   a smelly shuffle

towards   hot water   weak water   grimy.

A bowl of it.

Gone.

Bread. Bite. Gone.

Spoken in matter-of-fact manner:

There he went, another young one, fool,

idiot, we didn't stop him. Slow. Stupid.

A bony child, sixteen, no more, up to the

huge black bastard serving soup, asking for more.

Stone mad. Famished mad. Up to that monster

serving...

Pause.

Before our eyes he killed him with one

blow of his ladle.

Pause.

Before our eyes.

Silence.

Scuttles back to his tunnel. Silence. Sees a fly.

Fly.

Listen here, fly. Listen.

Small brother. Tiny sister.

Do you love?

Pause.

Fly. Listen. How many eyes have you?

Is it seven you have?

Oh you cursed creature,

it would be merciful to kill you.

Pause.

A wing of yours is broken, you have problems
my friend.

It is a peril to have eyes.

Pause.

I have two too many. They see too much.

I want my eyes gone from me.

Pause.

Poor fly. How you suffer. So much to see around
and about.

Pause.

I have love for you in your predicament.

Silence.

I will eat you.

Pause.

Because I love you.

Blackout. In the darkness, the words strike.

| AXE | AXE | AXE |

    STONE STONE STONE

| AXE | AXE | AXE |

ROCK HARD   STONE HARD

ROCK HARD   STONE HARD

ROCK HARD   STONE HARD

ROCK HARD   ROCK HARD

ROCK HARD   ROCK HARD

Saw. Suddenly saw

the guard slice,

with a swipe of his spade,

slice his arm off.

AXE   AXE   AXE

STONE   STONE   STONE

AXE   AXE   AXE

SWIPE SLAM   SPADE SLAM SLAM

SLAIN

DEAD DOWN DAMNED DOWN DEAD

STONE DEAD

Hate hate hate

foul

filth

dirt

HATEHATEHATEHATEHATE

SHITEFILTHFOULSHITEFILTH

FIST FACE FIST FACE FIST

Fist in his face

FACE INTO FLESH

Mimes punching the guard in the face then being struck by the guard and dying.

He struck me unto my death.

Felled me

as a slow tree

arching down

carrying growth with me.

How long I hang.

I have time to say goodbye,

all the time in the world,

leaving it to you

it is your problem.

I can see swallows

on their wires,

all going now.

To the chickens.

Chuck chuck chuck chuck,

My hungry ones.

Here's grain, here's meal, here's corn.

Never fret, never worry

all must be well.

Take your fill, take your pick,

take,

eat eat eat.

Moves downstage and climbs into the pile of clothes and rags.

There.

Here.

This is the place.

Here I belong.

Here I am with myself.

I can climb into it.

This is how it feels.

Simple. Slow. Quiet.

Present.   Certain.

Not a bother on me.

Here I am. Here it is.

My suit of clothes.

Ready and waiting.

In time. Correct.

Now I know the meaning of that word.

Correct. Never liked it until now.

Sounded like a slap.

How up to date this is. Modern.

Fashionable, a la mode, chic, complete.

I climb into myself and, sleep.

Enjoyable sleep.

This is the sleep I desire.

This is right.

This is fitting.

It is right and fitting.

The fitting is right.

He lies still, he is dying. Sings.

> Run rabbit, run rabbit, run, run, run,
> Don't let Hitler have his fun, fun, fun.
> He'll get by, without his rabbit pie,
> So run rabbit, run rabbit, run, run, run.

Lights down slowly.

Three

Les Yeux

Characters

All parts played by one man and one woman.

SUZANNE — A French woman living in Jersey, a resistance worker, step-sister to Lucy.

LUCY — Surrealist photographer, writer, artist.
Both she and her sister work their own resistance, they are 'the soldiers without a name.'

THE EYE — The watcher, male voice over.

NAZI ONE

NAZI TWO

THE ABORTION

THE BIG BAD WOLF

BETRAYER ONE

BETRAYER TWO

KURT	German soldier who works in the resistance. Voice-over.
NAZI UNIFORM	Voice-over.
NURSE	Voice-over.

Scene One

A Nazi uniform hangs on a cross upstage. Downstage a pile of objects including a chaise longue, chair etc. Clearly visible under the chaise longue is an Underwood typewriter and a wireless. Large chest downstage centre.

As audience enters, voice-over of a Nazi soldier telling the crowds to get ready for deportation.

VOICE-OVER

> Please proceed to your assembly point immediately. Please have your documents ready for inspection. Will all those with the family name beginning with A to G, please assemble in line A. Remember that it is only possible to bring one case per person travelling.
>
> *Silence.*
>
> Will all those with family name starting with H up to and including R, please assemble in line B. You may only bring one small case per adult travelling. You may not travel with more luggage than the permitted one case per adult.
>
> *Silence.*
>
> Will those travelling with family name starting

with the letter S up to and including Z, assemble in line C. It is only possible to bring one case per adult travelling. Any excess baggage will be confiscated. Proceed to your assembly points at once. Embarkation is commencing immediately.

Repeat as many times as appropriate, or until audience is assembled.

Spot on THE EYE only as THE EYE lights up.

THE EYE is free-standing and lights up internally.

Dead silence.

THE EYE

There is always an eye watching.

Without voice.

I keep a view on things.

I am behind you when you know not.

My profile is low.

The impartial and independent observer is so necessary for an ordered society.

Lights down.

Scene Two

Lights up on the two women putting up a banner in St Brelade's Church reading: 'Jesus ist gross aber Hitler ist grosser,' which translates as 'Jesus is great but Hitler is greater.' [1] *One of them on a ladder. Low lighting. Sound of haunting Satie piano music. Both women wear masks.*

They work swiftly and in silence, working as an efficient team. Their movements are contrapuntal to the music to convey efficiency/sadness. They take bunches of flowers and dip them in red paint. They then bring on, and set up, simple wooden crosses. On these crosses they write: 'For them the war is over.' Or it could already be written on the crosses. Freeze, holding crosses. Move to large chest and look at each other and give the thumbs-up sign. Music stops. Freeze. They take off masks.

Lights up.

They now put on Nazi uniforms and turn downstage to become looters and, rummaging in the chest, mime finding different objects.

NAZI ONE

    I think this might be an antique.

---

1   A translation of the original Cahun banner read 'Jesus is great but Hitler is greater, for Jesus died for men whereas men die for Hitler.'

NAZI TWO

>You must be joking!

NAZI ONE

>I like it anyway, it has character. Reminds me of home.

NAZI TWO

>Look at this book of beautiful old prints. Anatomical studies. These two crazy females. Never believe they were in the resistance. Did you see some of the photographs? Ultra modern stuff. But this book, exquisitely done, such craftsmanship. Nothing to compare with it nowadays. I think it might even be a first edition. If it's left in an empty house anything could happen to it.

NAZI ONE

>*Laughs.*
>
>Oh yes, anything at all could happen. Another radio, what fools risking their lives for a radio. Would you do that?

NAZI TWO

>*Pause.*
>
>I dunno. This typewriter has seen better days.

NAZI ONE

> Better catch this lot soon. They've some cheek. Putting that up in a church.

NAZI TWO

> No respect. That's blasphemy.
>
> *They end the scene by climbing the ladder and taking down the banner, throwing it on the pile of clothes. The ladder can be taken off stage with them when they exit or be thrown on the pile.*
>
> *Exit.*
>
> *Spot on crosses. Then lights down on crosses and spotlight up on THE EYE.*
>
> *Silence.*

THE EYE

> How I love silence.
>
> How much goes on in it.
>
> A million screams.
>
> *Pause.*
>
> Sshhhh
>
> *Lights up on LUCY and SUZANNE. They mime taking photos of each other. LUCY says 'click' for each photo. LUCY takes a photo of SUZANNE. Automatic photo of them both. LUCY*

on her own, automatic. LUCY takes SUZANNE at typewriter. LUCY takes photo of empty stage. LUCY exits. Empty stage, sound of photo taken.

Scene Three

Enter LUCY and SUZANNE on bicycles, circle the stage, stop either side, downstage left and right.

LUCY

>Once upon a time there were two sisters who were not sisters.

SUZANNE

>Half-sisters, as it were.

LUCY

>Not even half-sisters.

SUZANNE

>Stepsisters. But it is no one's business but ours.

LUCY

>Quite right. It's nobody's business.
>
>*They cycle around.*

SUZANNE

Picks up a hoe.

Weeds, weeds, weeds. Always seem to do so well.

LUCY

You can't kill a bad thing.

SUZANNE

Look at the Jerries.

LUCY

Weeds are just plants we find inconvenient.

SUZANNE

You don't do the hoeing. What a mess.

LUCY

There is always mess. I enjoy mess.

SUZANNE

Huh.

LUCY

If I have mess, then I can find order. A new order!

SUZANNE

Disorder.

LUCY

>Wild order. Another order. Search out the pattern, to detect a new order that you can't quite perceive. What is order?

SUZANNE

>I'm off down the garden, to make my order. So we can eat!
>
>*She gardens, hoes.*

LUCY

>I'll order beans. Haricots verts.
>
>*Returning to the story.*
>
>The sisters were not related as they shared no parent.

SUZANNE

>Better than being sisters. Stepsister always sounds bad. Wicked.

LUCY

>They could be ruder about their relations. But I want to tell a story: Two sisters came from la belle France. Over the sea they did dance to the sweet isle of Jersey.

SUZANNE

>Which they have no intention of leaving.

LUCY

> They didn't give a serious hoot about the Jerries. *Serious.*
>
> They were essentially against nationalism, separatism, that is against war. They would not move for any little Jerry.

SUZANNE

> We give a few hoots now and then, when we have famine.

LUCY

> Don't spoil my story.

SUZANNE

> May the war end quickly so we can get on with our lives and have some peace.

LUCY

> Ah peace. What is peace? Well, the two sisters lived in peace and harmony.

SUZANNE

> Harmony!

LUCY

> They loved their home and their work and their island. They spoke fluent English so pas de

problem. Then, one day, out of the sea and sky came, the Big Bad Wolf.

SUZANNE

Wolves.

LUCY

Packs of 'em.

LUCY and SUZANNE put on wolf masks. Sing 'Who's afraid of the big bad wolf.' March and give the Nazi salute. Sound of troops marching. Air raid warnings and news are heard over the following.

LUCY

The wolves came ranting and raging and marching and deporting, shooting, doing all the predictable things wolves do. But this is unfair on real wolves, they are loyal and intelligent animals who...

SUZANNE

In a fairy story you can't have those subtleties.

LUCY

The evolution of war has very little subtlety, resistance to war is a different matter.

But, the two sisters had a strong magic that could defeat the Big Bad Wolves with clever tricks.

SUZANNE

Not quite defeat, sort of give a few pin pricks.

LUCY

And what do you think this powerful spell was made of?

SUZANNE

Eye of newt and toe of frog.

LUCY

Sounds like our diet at the moment, I haven't had the smell of a frog's leg since...

SUZANNE

Stop. The rule.

LUCY

Sorry. You're right, no food talk. Now let me tell you the magic they had. Their magic was called a brain,

Pause.

a sense of humour and art.

SUZANNE

Very precious commodities.

LUCY

>	And a bicycle.

SUZANNE

>	Two bicycles.

LUCY

>	They were resourceful. But wait. Hear more…
>
>	Their spell, their spell,
>
>	of these two un-weird sisters hand in hand.
>
>	Mistresses of their house and land.

SUZANNE

>	Thus they turned about, about,
>
>	Took their little wireless out.

LUCY

>	How they twiddled knobs to hear
>
>	English voices calm and clear
>
>	Pour out the news.

SUZANNE

>	That was how they kept the score
>
>	Of what was happening in the war.

THE EYE

>	Ha!

SUZANNE and LUCY mime listening to the wireless. Give war news bulletins, make noises of noisy radios. Mime typing of messages on tissue paper to The Typewriter music. LUCY mimes being a soldier. SUZANNE mimes putting a tissue in LUCY's pocket.

LUCY

>This was a simple way to choose
>
>To catch the Germans as they
>
>Snoozed mentally, not alert.
>
>*Pick up bicycles.*

SUZANNE

>On their bicycles the sisters go
>
>Sometimes fast and sometimes slow
>
>In their nice and neat disguises.
>
>*Put on different disguises.*

LUCY

>And so avoid nasty surprises.

SUZANNE

>The roads of Jersey they did go
>
>Mingling with the traffic flow.

LUCY

>   Innocent as ladies shopping

>   Messages they were deftly popping

>   Into unsuspecting pockets.

>   Alarm! They cried

SUZANNE

>   In faultless German

LUCY

>   Encouragement to insurrection.

SUZANNE

>   In their pockets soldiers find

>   Rolls of tissue to unwind. Thin

>   As any holy wafer, imparting news to

>   Hit their minds.

LUCY

>   News the Reich did not impart, that

>   the war was off the mark,

SUZANNE

>   In fact the Allies had begun

>   To get the Jerry on the run.

LUCY

>   So they urged a change of heart

A change of mind, Nazi oppression

Throw behind

SUZANNE

And join with them to speed the day

Of Freedom, Peace and Liberty.

Women freeze. Dark. Spot on THE EYE.

THE EYE

Whispers.

I am the watcher.

So quiet. I do so much looking.

My patience is never ending.

Invisible. I became visible.

I remember and remember and remember.

Knowledge is power.

LUCY

The two sisters a faithful servant had.

SUZANNE

I don't think Hilda would think much of that description Lucy.

LUCY

This is my fairy story, you keep putting me off.

SUZANNE

> It's not grammatical...

LUCY

> This trusty servant... I can't think how to bring her in. Oh yes, I know, she can bring in the valiant steeds. You be Hilda bringing in the valiant steeds.

SUZANNE

> My God, neither I nor Hilda would go near any form of steed, trusty or otherwise.

LUCY

> So mounting my trusty steed.
> *Lucy straddles her bicycle.*

SUZANNE

> Bicycle.

LUCY

> Which hat this time? I think the nanny-look for me today.
> *They cycle singing 'Daisy, Daisy.' LUCY with her handful of tissue-paper messages, pushes her bicycle around the stage. SUZANNE puts on a Nazi uniform. Becomes NAZI ONE. Lighting*

*changes, makes big shadows from NAZI ONE.
LUCY approaches and puts a tissue in his
pocket, cycles away. This is repeated, NAZI ONE
becoming a different man, becoming more and
more surreal. Becomes wounded. Now without
a face. Now his face is a gun barrel, now it
becomes a pig, a rabbit etc. Moves downstage
and lighting casts huge shadows. LUCY exits.*

Scene Four

THE EYE

But I am always watching.

I am the voyeur.

Your movements are my pleasures.

I devour them. Your hidden deeds, my meat and drink. I will regurgitate them, one day, to my advantage.

LUCY enters downstage and stops, facing out towards the audience as if looking down from a high point, observing Jersey residents being deported to German war camps.

LUCY

>Looks just as bad from up here.
>
>*Pause.*
>
>Safe journey to you and back again.
>
>*SUZANNE joins her, pushing her bicycle.*

SUZANNE

>Quite a good day for our deliveries. Got rid of them all. Success. Oh my God, poor souls off to Germany. What hope for them?
>
>*Sea sounds. Ship's siren, gull cry.*

LUCY

>The Abortion was down there on the docks, looking smug.

SUZANNE

>He makes me vomit.

LUCY

>They were all so preoccupied with getting everyone on board the boat without any trouble. Made it easier for us.

SUZANNE

>They were edgy, I felt. They're getting the wind up. Makes them unpredictable.

LUCY

> Mrs Gould has gone.

SUZANNE

> Then that's why The Abortion looked so smug. He was all out to nail her. Pig.

LUCY

> Just for looking after that Russian kid. That did harm to no one. She's no spring chicken either. She's looking after another young chap on this trip did you see? The doctor tried to get her off but they're getting very bitchy, they smell defeat in the air.

SUZANNE

> Don't lose their touch, do they?
>
> *Pause.*
>
> It's easy to die where they are going.
>
> *Pause*
>
> Where we think they're going.

LUCY

> Know they're going.
>
> *Pause.*
>
> *LUCY and SUZANNE stand looking down.*

THE EYE

Faint strains of the deportees singing 'White Cliffs of Dover' are heard under THE EYE's speech.

What a lovely sunny day. Fair winds are set for France... Have I that quotation correct? Henry the Fifth of course, Shakespeare! What would we do without him.

I see. I see. The just and the unjust. What's the difference I ask myself? Who gives a toss. I put many on that boat.

Pause.

And other places.

SUZANNE

Let's go. I can't bear watching this.

LUCY

My blood does boil.

SUZANNE

This time it's them, the next could be us. If we'd been born in England this time would have been us.

Pause.

Vive La France.

LUCY

>They're singing, listen.

After a pause LUCY begins to join in with the departing deportees. They both sing 'White Cliffs of Dover.' Lights fade as LUCY and SUZANNE look out and sing. They then prop up their bicycles and move into the next scene.

Scene Five

SUZANNE is gardening as LUCY puts on a Nazi uniform that hangs on a cross upstage. Becomes a Nazi officer nicknamed THE ABORTION by the sisters. SUZANNE suddenly notices that THE ABORTION is standing there. She straightens up and talks to herself.

SUZANNE

>What are they doing in our garden? They're here at last. We've been expecting them almost daily for months. I feel like saying 'What took you so long?'
>
>*Addresses THE ABORTION.*
>
>Good evening.

THE ABORTION
> Good evening.
>
> *THE ABORTION stares like a waxwork. He bows from the waist.*
>
> German. Secret Police.
>
> *With great politeness.*
>
> We have come to search your house.

SUZANNE
> Come in...
>
> *Pause, adds with the forlorn hope that the word might engender gentleman-like behaviour in the officer.*
>
> Gentlemen.

THE ABORTION
> After you Madam.

SUZANNE
> My sister is not well, she is resting, please communicate with me and do not alarm her, she has a delicate disposition.

THE ABORTION
> I am most sensitive to disposition. I have a delicate nature myself.

Lights and music suggest an indoor scene. The scene changes slowly towards the surreal. Colour: purples and deep reds, orange and green. Purple faces, orange feet. Strobe lighting. Romantic music: 'We'll gather lilac in the spring again.' They waltz together, use the dance to exchange the greatcoat and hat, in a mock romantic dance.

THE ABORTION becomes LUCY again, SUZANNE becomes THE BIG BAD WOLF. She puts on wolf mask and LUCY puts on pig mask. Sits on the chaise longue.

THE BIG BAD WOLF

Little pig, little pig, can I come in?

LUCY

In pig mask.

No, no, by the hair of my chinny chin chin.

THE BIG BAD WOLF

Ho, ho, little pig. Then I'll huff and I'll puff and I'll huff and I'll puff and I'll huff and I'll puff and I'll blow your house in.

THE BIG BAD WOLF looms over LUCY who reclines on the chaise longue, in the pig mask, and smokes with a long cigarette holder.

LUCY

> Ah Monsieur le Commandant, forgive me for not rising, and that the curtains are drawn. I rest in a world of shadows. I am temporarily indisposed. I fear, because of the circumstances you and your countrymen impose on us, I cannot offer you refreshment, unless you'd care for a dish of potato peelings, which is what we look forward to with unbridled relish for our supper.

THE BIG BAD WOLF

> I have come to search your house.
>
> *Now getting down on hands and knees and sniffing out the typewriter and wireless.*

LUCY

> So this is not a social visit?

THE BIG BAD WOLF

> Not precisely.
>
> *Down on hands and knees.*
>
> Sniff, sniff, sniff.

LUCY

> Is it defeat he smells in the air?

THE BIG BAD WOLF

> I'm the fat cat

and you're the little mouse,

and I think there's cheese

in your little house.

On hands and knees sniffs out and finds the typewriter.

Sniff, sniff, sniff.

LUCY

Perching as a cat on the chaise longue.

Oh, Herr Cat

I am not your little mouse

so don't come a courting

in my little house.

THE BIG BAD WOLF

I'm not courting

you, says he. Your

actions can deny you

your life and liberty.

LUCY

Silly little puss

can't you see,

nothing is hidden

it's there for you to see.

> One fine day,
>
> we knew you'd come,
>
> that one fine day
>
> in the morning
>
> you'd stop our work and fun.

THE BIG BAD WOLF

> *Harshly, and standing up with a snarl.*
>
> Explain this!

LUCY

> It's a poor machine, some of the keys are quite worn. Look at the Q for instance. Can you type with more than two fingers? It must be so useful to do so.

THE BIG BAD WOLF

> Ah ha! This is as we expected. And the tissues?

LUCY

> We should never have trusted that tissue paper. Such rustly, gossipy stuff. But then it served us well and even with my typing, managing ten sheets at a time was a great advantage.
>
> *THE BIG BAD WOLF continues his sniffing and finds the wireless with no difficulty. Chases LUCY around the chaise longue.*

JERSEY LILIES

> Oh, greedy cat
>
> you may eat me,
>
> but even digested,
>
> poison I can be.

THE BIG BAD WOLF

> Ah ha! Your source of information.

LUCY

> My dear, how clever you are.
>
> When the cat's away, the mice do play.
>
> Pussy cat, pussy cat, where have you been?

THE BIG BAD WOLF

> What's that?

LUCY

> A ditty, a nursery rhyme.

THE BIG BAD WOLF

> Madam, you and I no longer inhabit the nursery.
> You do not appear to realise the seriousness of
> your situation.

LUCY

> We have something in common after all.

THE BIG BAD WOLF

> Madam, might I have the pleasure of escorting

>you. We have a delightful prison that I'm sure will do.
>
>*She accepts his invitation as if to dance. THE BIG BAD WOLF and LUCY sing and dance to the 'The Teddy Bears' Picnic,' the dance being an arrest. She ends in handcuffs.*

THE BIG BAD WOLF

LUCY

>If you go down to the woods today
>
>You're sure of a big surprise.
>
>If you go down to the woods today
>
>You'd better go in disguise,
>
>For every bear that ever there was
>
>Will gather there for certain because
>
>Today's the day, the Teddy Bears have
>
>Their picnic.
>
>*They dance off. Clang of doors. Lights down.*

Scene Six

THE BETRAYERS, wearing red noses, or two traditional theatre masks: happy for Nazi soldier, sad for LUCY, poke their heads up from behind the chest. They simper.

BETRAYER ONE

    I did feel I should say something

    I felt it my duty. I mean...

BETRAYER TWO

    They are odd women. They say they are
    eccentric. Well there's eccentric and eccentric.

BETRAYER ONE

    Kept themselves to themselves, that shows they
    were hiding something. Had money.

BETRAYER TWO

    Never short of a few bob.

BETRAYER ONE

    Now where did that come from? I said to my
    hubby I did. French. Not Jersey at all. Blow ins.

BETRAYER TWO

    They were only blow ins.

Both nodding in time together.

BETRAYER ONE

>Let them blow out, that's what I says.

Snigger.

BETRAYER ONE

BETRAYER TWO

>*Betrayers sing.*
>
>>It's a hap-hap-happy day
>>
>>Toodle doodle doodle aye,
>>
>>You can't go wrong
>>
>>If you sing a song,
>>
>>It's a hap-hap-happy day.
>
>*Remove clown noses etc. Both walk firmly to stage right and stage left and turn bicycles upside-down. Lights down or straight into scene seven.*

Scene Seven

A series of small meditations separated from one another to show the passing of time. SUZANNE moves into different poses that are simple and stark so forming a series of visual images that divide each of her speeches. One image could be without speech: light up and down, a deep black-and-white effect. It should develop a rhythm, the images stark and surreal. These pieces can overlap and repeat, become dream/nightmare/memory. As SUZANNE speaks LUCY could become one of her own creations, take photos. They deteriorate, become dirty, haggard.

Two bicycles on stage, upside-down. Light only on THE EYE.

THE EYE

> Ha. See what an observing eye can achieve. I, myself, on my own. My precise and painstaking observation over months. Years.
>
> Who killed Cock Robin?
>
> I, said the Spy, with my little eye,
>
> I killed Cock Robin.
>
> How satisfying to see a job well done.
>
> I have the eye for it!
>
> *Clang of doors. SUZANNE and LUCY are sitting behind the upturned bicycles. They look through the spokes of the wheels as if through bars of the prison. The wheels are spun, making shadows and tick, tick sounds, like the passing of time. They sit on the floor. Lights fade and are meagre. Both*

move in front of the bicycles into small squares of light that define their cells.

SUZANNE

The smell of disinfectant is heaviest on Friday and then decreases.

Lights change, she moves to make a new image. Clang of metal door. Light fades on SUZANNE and comes up on LUCY.

LUCY

I believe my first duty at present is to appear cheerful, to refrain from depressing everyone I am linked with. A superficial person would be liable to misinterpret this attitude.

Light fades on LUCY, very dim on SUZANNE. THE EYE glows.

SUZANNE

There is something strange and unnatural about an eye watching through the small round spy-hole. It is as if a fish were staring at you.

Light changes. New pose. Then spot on LUCY.

LUCY

Images. Images. So many images in my mind's

eye, to make, to photograph, to write. When? It's not only our bodies they starve.

Pause.

Time. The most precious gift. I will make an eye when we leave here. The all-seeing eye.

SUZANNE

Pacing out her cell.

I always thought there are two real luxuries in this overcrowded and busy world: time and space. Space I had in plenty and now I have lost it. But on the other hand I now have an awful lot of time to dispose of, such an invaluable commodity, always in short supply before this.

Pause.

It is up to me to make the most of it. I will try as far as I can to discard all preconceived ideas about prisons, warders, Germans and so on. I will live one day at a time and let our very uncertain morrow take care of itself.

Pause.

I am making New Year resolutions in midsummer!

New pose. She is still. LUCY takes an imaginary photograph.

LUCY

Click.

I have lived during the last years, and especially so during the last months and days, under what may be a delusion, of course, in the belief that I had reached at last a maturity that could be translated into words and convey a useful message to mankind. It is of course a somewhat un-English affirmation.

SUZANNE

In a new pose.

How easily the veneer of civilization will crack.

Pause.

Life seems like water. Apply new pressures, block up the accustomed outlets, and the whole fluid mass will push against the framework of society, probing for weak points and finding them.

Silence. Poses only. LUCY standing. Clang of doors. Change of pose. Colour purple.

LUCY

> *Sits.*
>
> An eye that is a face. A good eye? An evil eye? A neutral eye? Can an eye be neutral? I do not like this eye. But I will control it. When it opens and when it shuts. What it sees and what it does not see.
>
> *She gets up to retrieve a letter that has been hidden in a magazine and pushed under her door. It is a letter from KURT, she reads it. Sound of marching feet. Change of image. SUZANNE turns the wheel. Sits back to audience. Spot on THE EYE only.*

THE EYE

> I keep an eye on things, someone must see! I have a responsibility to the powers that be. I only report on facts. I am quite disinterested. I have the good of the whole community at heart. If there were more of us in the world it would be a better place. But what can I do, I ask you? Just my poor best.

LUCY

> Dear Friends,

This is to ask you to let me know your address as soon as possible. I am leaving this gaol and returning to my battery... I believe that we agree about politics, we are fighting the same enemy.

KURT

Voice-over.

I want to help and do what I can, that is why I ask you to trust me. If you will write letters to your parents or friends and tell me what political directions you wish to give, I shall deliver everything myself. It would be a good thing anyway that I might speak to your friends about the condition in this gaol. Your good friend, Kurt.

SUZANNE

When I hear people say: The only good German is a dead German, it always reminds me of the pub called 'The Quiet Woman Inn.' The sign of which so clearly implies that the only quiet woman is a dead woman. And naturally being a woman, I object to it.

Live whistle. Both go to centre stage and walk in a circle as if exercising in a prison yard. THE

*EYE watches. Letter from KURT is passed by
LUCY to SUZANNE.*

Whistle. They return to cells. Clang of doors.

KURT

Voice-over as SUZANNE reads.

When I am free I shall do what I can for you. As to food, I have not got much myself, but there are many other things one can do.

Be careful of the soldiers. Especially those in my cell. Let me have your answer on Tuesday, folded in this illustrated paper, under your door. Kurt.

SUZANNE change of pose.

SUZANNE

I have no quarrel with death. It is a friendly hand held out in the dark, and that knowledge is a good safeguard against fear and despair.

Clang of doors. Footsteps.

Scene Eight

LUCY puts cross with Nazi uniform on it, near chair and THE EYE. LUCY from her cell, with back to audience, becomes NAZI ONE. SUZANNE moves to chair in spotlight. She is being interrogated. SUZANNE in spotlight. NAZI ONE in shadow.

NAZI ONE

>*Speaks almost apologetically.*
>
>What I don't understand is: why do you hate us so much?

SUZANNE

>But I don't.
>
>*NAZI ONE looks surprised and unbelieving.*
>
>I am not a good hater anyway and I could never hate a nation as a lump. But I do think it is time you learned to make the best of the land you own instead of invading your neighbours' countries.

NAZI ONE

>It was a dangerous thing to do, to keep those guns, you might have shot us when we came to your house.

SUZANNE

>*Shakes her head and with a hint of regret.*
>
>That would have surprised me very much.

NAZI ONE

>*Loudly*

>Why?

SUZANNE

>I think I would have to be beside myself with fear or anger before I tried to kill a man. When you came to search our house, I was extremely annoyed, but I was neither afraid nor angry.

>*NAZI ONE frowns at her, concentrating, then suddenly stops frowning. During the following, LUCY becomes herself again and returns to cell.*

THE EYE

>How civilized.

>How we keep order.

>Disorder is so destructive and barbaric. The niceties keep us balanced. I am interested in the balanced view. Cool and calm brings contentment.

>*Spot on LUCY in her cell. She has become more haggard.*

LUCY

>Nothing but walls. And The Eye. I'll photograph walls.

She makes to take photographs.

Click. I will discover the geometry of walls. Click. The landscape of walls. The anatomy of walls. I will penetrate walls. Click. I will penetrate walls. Click. I will penetrate time. Click.

Silence.

I have no time at all. This time I have is dead time. Click. I record dead time.

Pause.

My photos come out blank,

Change of pose. Either voice-over from the NAZI UNIFORM or LUCY turns to become voice of the the NAZI UNIFORM interrogator.

NAZI UNIFORM

> *Bitterly.*

> You have given us much work.

SUZANNE

> It's very kind of you to say so. It was one of the results we hoped to achieve, and it is always nice to know that one has not worked in vain.

NAZI UNIFORM

> Are you sorry for what you have done?

SUZANNE

> You speak as if I had broken a teacup.
>
> *Pause.*
>
> Our propaganda was work, deliberately undertaken and pursued for over three years. If I could have any regrets I would have not bothered to do it.

LUCY becomes herself again.

LUCY

> Walls are all I have. I will have to learn to love them. It is their nature to stand still. They are as pathetic as I am. We cannot move or change ourselves. Nothing but stone walls. Dirty walls. Click. My lens pierces the wall and finds? Click, finds and finds. The sea – click – finds – my cat – click – finds – click –
>
> *Turns camera on audience. Sings.*
>
>> Vive l'amour, vive l'amour,
>>
>> Vive la compagnie.
>
> *Spot on SUZANNE. LUCY turns.*

NAZI UNIFORM

> Did you realise that this propaganda could undermine the German soldiers' moral?

She blinks at him in surprise, then realises that he is just asking a list of questions he has been told to ask.

SUZANNE

That is exactly what we were doing it for.

NAZI UNIFORM

So you would say you are responsible for your actions?

SUZANNE

From a legal point of view, certainly.

NAZI UNIFORM

Did you think that England would reward you for your work?

SUZANNE

Goodness.

Pause.

Since the Germans have overrun the island my concept of the future has been very limited. I make plans about what to grow and how to obtain what I cannot grow. I haven't thought about that, because I never believed we could survive the war.

NAZI UNIFORM

> Germany is the only country which shows gratitude to those who work for her.
>
> *Clang of doors. Light change on LUCY. She turns so she now appears in her cell as LUCY, or the voice of NAZI UNIFORM, during the following passage according to lighting changes.*

LUCY

> It seems to me that artists are unqualified to play any leading part in the revolution proper. They play a humble part like any citizen, but they should play a leading part which is their very own.
>
> *Pause.*
>
> They have to prefigure the highest aims of revolution. They have to be the severe keepers of those aims.
>
> *Lights change, spot swings to SUZANNE*

NAZI UNIFORM

> I have been looking over your file this morning and I realise we haven't got your religion.

SUZANNE

> *Surprised at the irrelevance of the matter.*
>
> Does it matter?

NAZI UNIFORM

> One always puts down religion. There is a space provided for it.

SUZANNE

> Oh.
>
> *Pause. To herself.*
>
> Technically I am a Roman Catholic, having been baptized in infancy and confirmed at the ripe age of ten. But years of what the Lycée called 'preparation religieuse' has no more made a Christian of me than eight years' piano lessons has made me a musician.
>
> *To NAZI UNIFORM.*
>
> You better put me down as agnostic.

NAZI UNIFORM

> But I cannot do that!

SUZANNE

> Why not?

NAZI UNIFORM

> Because one never does it! Everyone has a religion.

SUZANNE

> Have they?
>
> *Interested.*
>
> Have you got one?

NAZI UNIFORM

> Certainly. I am a Catholic.

SUZANNE

> That is very curious.

NAZI UNIFORM

> *Loudly with controlled indignation.*
>
> Why is it curious?

SUZANNE

> *Meekly.*
>
> I don't want to offend you, but it seems to me that the qualities required of a good Christian are not the same as those of an efficient member of the Gestapo.
>
> *To herself.*

I can see the sun outside and they keep me away from it. It's hateful.

Clang of doors. Both walk back to prison cells. LUCY receives another letter.

I feel at times a curious happiness due to the fact I am relieved of all responsibilities. It is rather shocking, but then there is nothing wrong in being happy. So I just enjoy it when it happens.

LUCY reads the letter from KURT. His voice is heard on voice-over while SUZANNE attempts to slit her wrists.

KURT

Dear Friends,

Here again a few lines.

Perhaps you can do something for me... I would very much like to speak for a few minutes with the English C.O. in Jersey, or with any other officer. You know that I have much to tell. Try to do this for me, for your way was also my way and we have withstood even through the darkest hours. For this, four of my comrades had to die. I must stop now. God bless your King and the United Nations with liberated Europe.

I hope you both are well. I had no idea

how things were before I came here. The oberfeldwebel who was arrested as a deserter has been shot. Please think of me, Kurt.

Sound of prisoners singing. LUCY is writing a letter.

LUCY

Mere hints, scraps, reach outside about our life here, which is at once nightmare-ish, and quite sordid most of the time, but with the priceless compensation of solidarity, at its best, a kind of of paradise.

Music: a snatch of 'White Cliffs of Dover.' The women stand in their separate cells and join in.

SUZANNE

In a way it is much easier to adjust myself to the idea of death than to the idea of survival. It is so much more simple.

LUCY

Writing.

Patriotism can only have one meaning for me, my love of a national culture. Nothing to do with a government or pride in the past, that is what I am against. From the French I have learned a love of beauty and truth, the value of moral courage unto death and to keep ever an open mind. From the English I have learned the necessity to overcome doubts in the fight against evil.

SUZANNE

What a stubborn thing life is. No doubt it has to be, with the thousand and one things that can go wrong in a human body.

THE EYE swivels and stares at her. SUZANNE draws a red line around each wrist with a felt pen and draws the line on down to the centre of her palm to make a red stigmata mark.

LUCY

Writing.

I feel so fed up with everything this evening that it needs all the spirit of fraternity of this place to pull me out of hatred's hell... What a system eh? Isn't worth dying against. But what for?

SUZANNE

The blood simply goes on dripping from my finger tips. What I want to see is it welling out from the wrist with each pulsation.

THE EYE slowly shuts. LUCY turns the bicycle wheel.

Voice-over.

I was beginning to drift away to that unforgettable feeling of detachment I knew thirteen years ago when I had been given an injection of Pentothal before an operation.

VOICE OF NURSE

Voice echoey and loud.

You must be sorry for those poor young soldiers who are in prison for what you have done.

SUZANNE

Voice-over while SUZANNE slowly bandages both of her arms.

I never liked Herr Grosse Doktor. I like him even less now I've just heard that he went to our house and stole two portfolios of beautiful old anatomical charts that my father used as a student seventy years ago.

Scene Nine

Sound of slamming doors, feet on stone.

LUCY

SUZANNE

>Ding Dong Bell
>
>Pussy's in the well
>
>All the judge and jury said was

LUCY

>You will go to Hell

SUZANNE

>Ding Dong Bell

LUCY

SUZANNE

>Ding Dong Bell,
>
>Good girls down the well.
>
>You've been bold and naughty girls,
>
>So you'll go hell.
>
>Ding Dong Bell.

SUZANNE

> *With clown mask and Nazi hat.*
>
> I say, I say, I say,
>
> what did the judge say to the prisoner?

LUCY

> *In clown mask.*
>
> I say, I say, I say, I don't know,
>
> What did the judge say to the prisoner?

SUZANNE

> Down on your knees,
>
> Have a little cry,
>
> Plead with them for mercy,
>
> You're too young to die.

LUCY

> Say you'll be a goody,
>
> Sign on the dotted line.
>
> Say you'll just do anything
>
> For time, time, time.

SUZANNE

> Do a little grovel,

You know the kind of thing.

If you want some supper

You must sing, sing, sing.

I say, I say, I say,

Surely one can always ask for mercy?

LUCY

No.

SUZANNE

No.

LUCY

No.

SUZANNE

No.

LUCY

No. We can't. Never. It does not matter much when you are fighting an ordinary war. But we are fighting on ideological grounds and so it is quite impossible.

Scene Ten

Spot on THE EYE. THE EYE is wearing a judge's wig. Turns to face the audience. Sound of a judge's gavel. The two women do a little dance in time with THE EYE's sentencing.

Repeat as above. I say, I say, I say...

THE EYE

An appropriate sentence of death.

Hammer sound on death. THE EYE winks.

A sympathetic sentence of death.

Hammer sound on death. THE EYE winks.

A seasonal sentence of death.

Hammer sound on death. THE EYE winks.

A reasonable sentence of death.

Hammer sound on death. THE EYE winks.

An infinitely practical, complete and tactical, successful sentence of death.

Hammer sound on death. THE EYE winks.

Death. Death. Death. Death.

Hammer on each 'death,' THE EYE stares straight ahead. Silence. LUCY and SUZANNE return to cells. Music: 'Somewhere Over the Rainbow.'

Spot off THE EYE. LUCY back in her cell pacing up and down.

LUCY

Now I believe I know, the nearest I can state is that revolution is a permanent characteristic of mankind.

SUZANNE receives and reads letter from KURT. KURT'S voice on voice-over.

KURT

Dear Friends,

I beg you to understand me, for I must help you, whatever it may cost me. Already in France I have done much for England. It was my duty. From the very beginning I knew that Hitler meant to conquer the world in a criminal way. First there was that shameful persecution of the Jews which I thought worst of all. I would like nothing better than to be able to talk freely with you. Destroy the letters I send you. I do the same with yours.

Kurt

SUZANNE

> I don't find the idea of death frightening. Of course I may be afraid when the time comes. I cannot tell.

THE EYE

> Ding Dong Bell,
>
> Pussy's in the well,
>
> And my nose is telling me
>
> She begins to smell.
>
> *Giggles. Blackout. Both women turn bicycle wheels.*

Scene Eleven

Lights up on LUCY writing her letter.

LUCY

> S told me she gave you a little account of our trial. I would like to give an idea of the atmosphere of it, but it is not possible. Unless I survive, which is unlikely.
>
> *Pause.*
>
> Remember, dear Kurt, you are not supposed to

have seen us, nor of course heard anything about
our state of destitution or the trial. I am writing
at dawn and dusk mostly, for security's sake.
Now it is almost dark. I can hardly read over
what I have written you. Whatever it is, it has to
stand as it is, with many mistakes. But I want you
to know that my greatest suffering is the anxiety
about the friends I might, through my rashness,
have got into trouble. However all this has to be
overcome. Bless you, dear Kurt... Lucy.

Slow fade of lights.

Scene Twelve

Change of light for liberation. Sound of church bells, cheering crowd, singing. The women jump up and ride bicycles around the stage, wave, sing with the imaginary crowd, sing 'Run Rabbit Run' and 'We're Gonna Hang Out the Washing on the Siegfried Line.' Freeze downstage, put down bikes.

LUCY

> But.
>
> So the Tommies saved the day,

And landed in St Helier's bay,

And marched the Nazi troops away.

SUZANNE

And saved our bacon

Hip, hip, hooray.

LUCY

We can die another day.

Time has had a little stay

Freedom has kept death at bay.

SUZANNE

For this season.

LUCY

But

This is a story I was telling,

The once upon a time... and is there a happy ending...?

SUZANNE

We all have stories, true and partly so.

LUCY

The dream more true than the reality.

SUZANNE

>   The reality invaded by myth.

LUCY

>   The reality respected through memory,
>
>   memory transformed to make the story.

SUZANNE

>   We are our story, this is our happy ending.

LUCY
SUZANNE

>   *Sing.*
>
>   >   Now we all come out to play,
>   >
>   >   The moon doth shine as bright as day.
>   >
>   >   Leave your supper and leave your sleep
>   >
>   >   And join your playfellows in the street.
>   >
>   >   Come with a whoop, come with a call,
>   >
>   >   Come with a goodwill, or not at all.
>   >
>   >   Up the ladder and down the wall,
>   >
>   >   A halfpenny roll will serve us all.
>   >
>   >   You find milk and I'll find flour,
>   >
>   >   And we'll have pudding in half an hour.

Music: Satie.

THE EYE

> *Lights up.*
>
> You're not heroes.
>
> Forget it. No one will remember you. You are erased.
>
> *Lights fade on the women, remain on THE EYE.*
>
> Those goddamn whores disintegrating in the briny. Ha. All will forget you. Remember those bones piled high in Dachau? Empty suitcases. Those fellows' bodies behind the walls in the hospital, good insulation! Nothing wasted. I like that. Goody, goody. A job well done. Just my style.
>
> Your words, your works, nothing. Lost in empty attics. They have no significance. Photographs? Forget it. Bizarre wanderings of a diseased mind. Hysterical women. So many men on my side I have hardly a job to do. Mine's a good life. I have a wish for you. I am a simple fellow. I like the quiet life. I wish peace for you.
>
> Peace to all men.

Spot on THE EYE.

Click, sound of photo being taken.

Music: Satie.

Lights down on THE EYE, fade up on LUCY and SUZANNE who stand still, look at each other. Turn slowly, walk back to the chest, close the chest doors, turn front, look at each other, look out front, lights fade slowly.

Acknowledgements

The following songs are featured in the play:

Run Rabbit Run by Noel Gay and Ralph Butler, 1939;

White Cliffs of Dover by Walter Kent and Nat Burton, 1941;

Hey Little Hen by Noel Gay and Ralph Butler, 1941.

Will You Remember by Sigmund Romberg and Rida Johnson Young, 1917;

Who's Afraid of the Big Bad Wolf by Frank Churchill and Ann Ronell, 1933;

Daisy, Daisy by Harry Dacre, 1890;

The Teddy Bears' Picnic by John Walter Bratton and Jimmy Kennedy, 1932;

It's a Hap-hap-happy Day by Sammy Timberg, Winston Sharples and Al J. Neiburg, 1939;

Vive La Compagnie, traditional music of unknown author;

We're Gonna Hang Out the Washing on the Siegfried Line by Lesley Sarony and Lesley Holmes, 1940;

The Typewriter arranged by Leroy Anderson, 1950.

www.ingramcontent.com/pod-product-compliance
Lightning Source LLC
Chambersburg PA
CBHW070954080526
44587CB00015B/2300